✠

*Holy Week
Sonnets*

✠ ✠ ✠

To Hugh McKenna,

Whose spirit in worship
ministered to me,
Philip Rosenbaum
April 3, 2005

✚ ✚ ✚ ✚ ✚ ✚ ✚
✚ ✚ ✚

Holy Week Sonnets

✚ ✚
✚

Philip Rosenbaum

POSTERITY PRESS

© 2004 Philip Rosenbaum
Printed in the United States of America
All Rights Reserved

ISBN 1-889274-21-6

All scripture quotations, unless otherwise indicated,
are taken from the Holy Bible, New King James Version.
Copyright ©1982 by Thomas Nelson, Inc.
Used by permission. All rights reserved.

Library of Congress Cataloging-in-Publication Data

Rosenbaum, Philip.
  Holy week sonnets / Philip Rosenbaum.
    p. cm.
  Includes bibliographical references.
  ISBN 1-889274-21-6 (alk.paper)
    1. Jesus Christ—poetry. 2. Christian poetry, American.
  3. Holy Week—Poetry. 4. Sonnets, American. I. Title.

PS3618.O83165H65 2004
811'.6—dc22

POSTERITY PRESS, INC.
P.O. Box 71081
Chevy Chase, MD 20813
www.posteritypress.com

*To Costas and Louise Chrissos,
my parents in law and in love*

When for the thorns with which I long, too long,
    With many a piercing wound,
    My Saviour's head have crown'd,
I seek with garlands to redress that wrong . . .

                              ANDREW MARVELL
                              The Coronet

And if thy holy Spirit, my Muse did raise,
Deigne at my hands this crown of prayer and praise.

JOHN DONNE
La Corona

Contents

Foreword by Joni Eareckson Tada x

The Lord Who Lives 3
A Single Stone 5
The Burden 7
The Olive Press 9
The Scholar 11
And Jesus Stood 13
Good Friday, 1987 15
Good Friday, Flying Eastward 17
The Man Who Walked 19
The Men Who Knew 21
The Signature 23
The Old Man's Prophecy 25
Keystone 27
The Witness 29
The Curtain 31
The Hiding Place 33
Where He Was Crucified 35

I Lay in Darkness 37
Deathwatch 39
Who Told Saint Matthew? 41
I Did Not Weep 43
The Bible Study (I) 45
The Bible Study (II) 47
The Epithet 49

Scripture Sources & Notes 51

Foreword

I may be a quadriplegic, but that does not slow me down. I live with my wheelchair on one speed—fast-forward. In a day, I may plow through several articles, tackle a pile of dictating, haggle through an executive meeting, correct a manuscript, juggle a few phone appointments, and then head for home long after we've closed our office doors at 5 P.M. Life is full and fast. Often too fast.

Maybe this is why I'm drawn to poetry. It's a way—some say the best way—to gear down the pace and . . . pause. Meandering through a collection of good poems is a way for the soul to breathe deeply, a chance to inhale and exhale celestial air with each rhythm and rhyme. To linger over a poem is to rise to a higher plane and engage the heart and mind in the hieroglyphics of heaven. It's a place I don't visit often enough.

But I did the other day.

My friend Philip Rosenbaum sent me his *Holy Week Sonnets*. I hardly got past the first few pages when I discovered afresh that the passion of Christ cannot be plowed through. You can't fast-forward through Maundy Thursday to Resurrection Sunday. Poetry may demand our intellect, but these poems command our undivided heart as well. *Holy Week Sonnets* speak to our innermost being, revealing the beauty and brilliance of our Savior in the most unexpected way. And, oh, how fresh the air of celestial conversation!

So thank you, dear reader, for *pausing*. Bless you for lingering on these poems. You are about to move from the outer courts to the inner, discovering anew just how holy the week of our Lord's passion really is.

Joni Eareckson Tada
Spring 2004

The Sonnets

Luke 10:38–42
John 12:1–8
Matthew 26:6–13

The Lord Who Lives

Because I was in love with Jesus Christ
(I wish the world could know the love we shared!)
I suffered persecution. When I cared
For nothing but His word, when it sufficed
My heart's desire (as a highly-priced
Fine pearl subdues the merchant who has dared
To risk all things for one)—my sister glared
Like Adam's firstborn when he sacrificed.
The day I broke my precious bottle of
Fine perfume—how the wolf aroused the sheep
To say that I was wasteful! Then I heard
The Lord who lives to vindicate true love,
Like the first wind which moved upon the deep,
Stir endless waves of comfort with a word.

Luke 10:38–42
John 12:1–2

A Single Stone

I WAS NOT BEAUTIFUL, BUT I COULD WORK.
And work I did, but not without distraction:
My lovely sister's idleness would irk
My soul, spoiling my hard-won satisfaction.
From Christ I learned that he who tends the vine
Or labors in the vat need not despise
The one who sits and savors the new wine:
Things look so different through the Master's eyes!
The whole world sees my sister's well-deserved
And lasting monument. But what of mine?
Not many notice it: "And Martha served"—
A single stone (one useful, though not fine)
In that great edifice no man could build,
The Church where service is a joy fulfilled.

Mark 11:1–11
Psalm 22:1, 7–8, 14–18
Psalm 69:19–21

The Burden

Unaccustomed to her burden, she knows not
That never beast bore such a Man as this,
Who meekly rides to His appointed lot,
A crown of thorns and a betrayer's kiss.
And never man will carry such a weight
As He bears now in this, His day of power,
Ascending toward a strait and narrow gate,
His agonizing last and finest hour.
She bravely struggles on, despite her fear
Of cheering men, whom He as gravely views
As an admiral watching distant storms draw near
To lash bright waves to dark and deadly hues;
He knows the death decreed in ancient psalms,
The Tree that looms beyond these scattered palms.

Matthew 26:36–38
Luke 22:44

The Olive Press

THEN JESUS CAME WITH THEM UNTO A PLACE—
Unto the garden of Gethsemane—
Where every cultivated olive tree
Must give its bitter fruit to the embrace
Of the relentless instrument of grace . . .
An instrument which feels the misery
Of brokenness, and groans in agony
Until it has expressed the final trace
Of fragrant oil to light the lamps of men.
He came there in the darkness of the night
To suffer pressures men could never know—
The Voice of God come walking once again
In garden paths—to feel poor Adam's plight,
The crushing weight of weakness and of woe.

1 Peter 1:18–19
Hebrews 5:8–9

The Scholar

A LAMB WITHOUT A BLEMISH OR A SPOT,
Mature yet tender, proper for the feast,
(Before its sinless blood might be released
And struck upon the doorway steaming hot)
Must stand examination. Wisdom got
Through long discrimination, and increased
By one more patient searching of the beast,
Shall know if it appear what it is not.
Perfect, but not perfected, incomplete,
The Lamb of God has something yet to learn:
Under severe instructors, He shall bleat
To satisfy the Principal so stern
His one omniscient Scholar must be beat
To gain His fools the prize they could not earn.

Matthew 27:11

And Jesus Stood

NOT ALL THE STAGES SET BY MORTAL HANDS
And decorated long and lavishly
To evoke the flavor of exotic lands—
And yet to do it with such subtlety
That men hear nothing but heroic speech,
Envision nothing but the lovers' kiss—
Whatever heights theatric art may reach,
They'll ne'er do justice to a scene like this.
The stage, the script, the lights, and all the skill
Of actors practiced till they could not err
Performed the Author-and-Director's will:
The moon paused in the path prepared for her;
The sun was silent; all the stars grew still—
And Jesus stood before the governor.

Revelation 1:5–6

Good Friday, 1987

Jesus, You know I do not understand
Your love, Your sacraments, Your sufferings,
Your grace exalting me with priests and kings
Reigning forever in the Promised Land.
I am a child who takes his father's hand
Walking along the beach, who while he clings
Fears not the surf, but begs a tale that brings
Him dreams of sailing far beyond the strand.
O tell me once again and I'll receive
The things I cannot know and count them true:
How if I were the only man to grieve
The heart of God, You'd take Your cross anew
(I do not understand, but I believe)
To die for me, that I might live for You.

Luke 23:44–46
Psalm 31:5

Good Friday, Flying Eastward

THE HOURS WHICH YOU SPENT UPON THE CROSS
Have flown from me; (I fly against the sun).
Morning I have, and evening; all my loss
Is midday. Just the time, Lord, when You won
The battle for my soul has been undone.
How should I have a portion in the fight
If that grim afternoon were not begun,
The time of darkness overwhelming light?
Where would I be if in Your holy sight
No sacrifice were offered for my sin,
If I should stand before You with no right
But merit of my own? Let the earth spin,
And let my daylight hours be short or long,
But save the moment that removes my wrong.

Genesis 22:6–8
Exodus 3:14
Mark 14:61–62

The Man Who Walked

THE MAN WHO WALKED WITH FIRE IN HIS HAND
Rose early, that his work might soon be done.
He took a knife, he took his only son
To a high mountain in a barren land.
As at first light the climber takes his stand
To spy a route (where men say there is none)
Far up the craggy peak which must be won,
The burdened son his burdened father scanned.
He wondered why (since they had been as one)
He seemed forbidding now and far away,
His clouded brow more hidden from the sun
Than regions sunk in shadow all the day.
   "Father, are you concerned about God's lamb?"
   "Knowing He will provide, my son, . . . I am."

Mark 12:7–8

The Men Who Knew

THERE IS A SCRIPTURE WHICH SO CHILLS MY SOUL
My fervent muse feels numb: "This is the heir."
Who would have dreamed that wicked men would dare
To think their machinations could control
The Son of God Himself?... That as they stole
From widows without consequence or care,
Now they would take Messiah in their snare
Like a helpless rabbit? Who in the whole
Recorded history of wickedness
Conceived of such a sin? Did man's delusion
Ever soar so high, or so far suppress
The voice of conscience to his own confusion?
   How could the wings of mercy spread above
   The men who knew they crucified God's love?

Luke 23:32–43
Matthew 20:1–9

The Signature

I MOCKED HIM WITH THE CRUCIFYING CROWD.
I mocked him; (What else was there to do
To dull the pain?) "Father, forgive them . . ." Who?
The soldiers surely. Did he mean the proud
And vengeful hypocrites who cried aloud,
"Come down and we'll believe"? Somehow I knew
His word was sown in me—and the seed grew,
Breaking the ground that never had been ploughed.
Though I had been an idler all the day,
He brought me to His vineyard at the last;
My feeble work, His overwhelming pay
(Now that our brief negotiating's past)
Seem less amazing than the wondrous way
He signed the contract that would bind us fast.

Luke 2:34–35
John 19:25–27

The Old Man's Prophecy

By the cross of Jesus His mother stood:
"Woman, behold your son!" At last, at last
Her years of secret wondering are past:
The Carpenter is tortured by the wood;
Grief God had hidden from her for her good
Now overwhelms and leaves her soul aghast,
Like the victim of a flood which came so fast
It swept away all shelter, friends, and food—
An aimless wanderer, haggard and gaunt,
All heedless of the pressing needs of life . . . .
The old man's prophecy no more will haunt
The gables of her mind: She feels the knife
(Which till today had only pricked her wonder)
Unsheathed at last, cutting her soul asunder.

John 19:28–30

Keystone

"It is finished!" His dying words evoke
Visions of long-awaited consummation:
The temporary scaffoldings (which cloak
The everlasting arches)—family, nation,
Empire—despite their strength and elevation,
Must be dismantled soon. Only a few
Rude passersby watch workmen at their station
Lifting the Keystone up. Ah! Would they hew
Its sacred sides so roughly if they knew
That pilgrims evermore would throng the place,
Bringing such treasures as they think are due
For radiant glass to glorify the grace,
And halls of polished marble to reflect
The soaring Spirit of the Architect?

Mark 15:39
Psalm 22:1, 7–8, 14–18

The Witness

D'you think it strange—with such a dreary job,
(To supervise another crucifixion,
To see the hardest men break down and sob,
And not to care if it is truth or fiction
They utter, when with dying men's conviction
They still maintain they have done nothing wrong)
And being ignorant of the prediction
King David made in sure prophetic song,
(Though all the Jews had studied it so long,)
Yet when it was fulfilled before our eyes,
By grace I knew it, and my faith grew strong
While they mocked on beneath the darkening skies—
    D'you think it strange that I am at a loss,
    Knowing the Man I put upon the Cross?

Matthew 27:41–51

The Curtain

Christ on the cross they mock, but do not cease
To keep a man on their well-rutted way,
Appeasing the Almighty day by day
Before the Veil—that great symbolic piece
Of purple, blue, and scarlet soft as fleece.
God's Son is dead. Will Adam's son then stay
In God's own house, as lighthouse keepers may,
Safe through a raging storm in light and peace?
Jerusalem is dark. He dimly sees
The Curtain torn, and the forbidden space
Naked before his eyes. Thrown down on knees
That tremble like the earth, afraid to face
His Maker, with averted eyes he flees
The dreadful sight of God's bare holy place.

Isaiah 32:1–2

The Hiding Place

As a man seeks shelter from a raging storm
Which breaks the cedars with its mighty thunder,
And stumbles on a cave secure and warm,
Where all his fear of lightning turns to wonder;
And as a frightened chick takes shelter under
His mother's wing and her sharp watchful eye,
From all who seek to tear his soul asunder,
From every silent predator on high;
And as a man is glad when he draws nigh
A great rock's shadow in a weary land,
And there takes shelter from the scorching sky,
And feels refreshed, but not by his own hand;
    From Satan's clouds and claws and heat I hide,
    Safe in the shelter of my Saviour's side.

John 19:38–42

Where He Was Crucified

Now in the place where He was crucified
There was a garden; and within the garden
A tomb, where two God-fearing men defied
The priests who gave a perfect Man no pardon.
And so it was, when men and times were grim,
Two timid hearts did prove their love was true:
With aloes and with myrrh they buried Him,
And where their hearts were placed their treasure too.
It's time for me to bring my precious spices
To honor Him who bravely died for me,
No more to hide in fear of sins and vices
From which so long ago He set me free.
    For He's the One who all my needs supplied;
    And I'm the place where He was crucified.

Psalm 139:11–12

I Lay in Darkness

I lay in darkness, feverish and chilled,
When she who loves me came to give me drink:
The doorway's glow my room so softly filled,
My eyes took in the light without a blink.
My hand responded to the inviting clink
Of glass and ice—when, lo, she passed me by!
I had been too insensitive to think:
She could not see, though I could see her try.
How glad I am that He who came to die
To free me from my darkness and disease
Came softly in the night to satisfy
My thirst, and brought His light to me with ease;
    Yet He saw well when all my room was dim,
    For light and darkness are the same to Him.

Matthew 28:1–15

Deathwatch

Those wicked men! The shining angel's face
They saw, like lightning, struck them full of fear.
They trembled like the earth as they drew near
Unto the gates of death—the very place
Where they'd blasphemed the Saviour of the race.
God showed them wondrous mercy; yet it's clear,
As they before the wicked one appear,
That gold means more to them than truth or grace.
From their hard hearts no angel rolls the stone;
But when I would dismiss them in disgust,
Angelic questions come: Have you not known
Indwelling sin's deceit? Has never lust
Found you its slave, who takes the tempter's bait
And revels in the deed he ought to hate?

Matthew 28:2

Genesis 8:8–9

Book of Common Prayer,
Collect for the Second Sunday in Advent

Who Told Saint Matthew?

WHO TOLD SAINT MATTHEW THAT THE ANGEL SAT
Upon the stone which he had rolled away?
The quaking soldiers, powerless to say,
"Be gone, Sir!"—or the rulers who begat
Lies all the people must have wondered at?
I hold the stone more likely to betray
What happened in the dawning of the day,
For it was softer and less obdurate.
It could have been that Watcher from above
Who noticed Noah reaching from the ark
To draw unto himself the restless dove;
The One who moved on Jonah in the dark
To pray to Him whose all-absorbing love
Digests each lesson we must learn and mark.

John 20:11–16

I Did Not Weep

I did not weep because I'd come so far;
I did not weep for all the gold I'd spent;
Nor did I weep as one who does repent
Hitching his earthly hopes unto a star
That will not rise again. Death cannot bar
A faithful dog from waiting where the scent
Reveals to him the way his master went—
No matter where his food and water are.
So I stood there and wept. Though men had cursed
And hurt me in the past, I did not fear
That they might come again and do their worst
To one who stood there trembling, weak, and wary;
But I was not at all prepared to hear
The Voice that said, "Let there be light"—say, "Mary!"

Luke 24:13–33

The Bible Study (I)

"O fools," the Stranger said, "and slow of heart,
Why do you not believe the sacred Word?"
We wondered why our dampened hearts concurred
So well with His rebuke, as not to part
Away from Him in pride, or seek to thwart
His teaching us a lesson. Then we heard
Things sensible to God, to us absurd—
And found ourselves enraptured from the start.
What caused our hearts to burn within us so?
It was not passion, though He passion brought.
It was not knowledge, though He made us know
The fate of One disguised, unknown, unsought.
He loved to rouse our wonder first—to show
In His own flesh the very thing He taught.

Luke 24:13–33

The Bible Study (II)

What made our dampened hearts within us burn?
His voice like distant thunder crashing still?
His gladness, like the all-embracing trill
Of birds rejoicing in the sun's return?
Sure something deep inside Him made us yearn,
Like lovers whose bright minds and bodies thrill
To shape themselves unto another's will—
But how or why they dare not to discern.
We only knew He carried us afar
To undiscovered regions of the soul,
Like wise men following an unknown star,
Beyond their destination, to their goal.
We saw the God who made Himself a man:
And back to dark Jerusalem we ran.

John 20:24–29

The Epithet

I COULD HAVE CURSED THE ERRAND I WAS ON,
The foolishness that kept me from my friends,
The separation due to petty ends
That once seemed lofty. Had I not been gone,
My troubled soul would never have been gnawn
By that devouring doubt, that softly rends
Believer from believer and expends
The soul's resources till they're all withdrawn.
I am not one to glory in my shame;
But as the facets of a gem are shown
Reflected by the foil that sits behind,
In faith I will receive my given name,
I'll bless the epithet by which I'm known—
That those who do not see may not be blind.

Scripture Sources & Notes

The Lord Who Lives

Luke 10:38–42

Now it happened as they went that He entered a certain village; and a certain woman named Martha welcomed Him into her house. And she had a sister called Mary, who also sat at Jesus' feet and heard His word. But Martha was distracted with much serving, and she approached Him and said, "Lord, do You not care that my sister has left me to serve alone? Therefore tell her to help me." And Jesus answered and said to her, "Martha, Martha, you are worried and troubled about many things. But one thing is needed, and Mary has chosen that good part, which will not be taken away from her."

John 12:1–8

Then, six days before the Passover, Jesus came to Bethany, where Lazarus was who had been dead, whom He had raised from the dead. There they made Him a supper; and Martha served, but Lazarus was one of those who sat at the table with Him. Then Mary took a pound of very costly oil of spikenard, anointed the feet of Jesus, and wiped His feet with her hair. And the house was filled with the fragrance of the oil. Then one of His disciples, Judas Iscariot, Simon's son, who would betray Him, said, "Why was this fragrant oil not sold for three hundred denarii and given to the poor?" This he said, not that he cared for the poor, but because he was a thief, and had the money box; and he used to take what was put in it. But Jesus said, "Let her alone; she has kept this for the day of My burial. For the poor you have with you always, but Me you do not have always."

Matthew 26:6–13

And when Jesus was in Bethany at the house of Simon the leper, a woman came to Him having an alabaster flask of very costly fragrant oil, and she poured it on His head as He sat at the table. But when His disciples saw it, they were indignant, saying, "Why this waste? For this fragrant oil might have been sold for much and given to the poor." But when Jesus was aware of it, He said to them, "Why do you trouble the woman? For she has done a good work for Me. For you have the poor with you always, but Me you do not have always. For in pouring this fragrant oil on My body, she did it for My burial. Assuredly, I say to you, wherever this gospel is preached in the whole world, what this woman has done will also be told as a memorial to her."

A Single Stone

Luke 10:38–42

Now it happened as they went that He entered a certain village; and a certain woman named Martha welcomed Him into her house. And she had a sister called Mary, who also sat at Jesus' feet and heard His word. But Martha was distracted with much serving, and she approached Him and said, "Lord, do You not care that my sister has left me to serve alone? Therefore tell her to help me." And Jesus answered and said to her, "Martha, Martha, you are worried and troubled about many things. But one thing is needed, and Mary has chosen that good part, which will not be taken away from her."

John 12:1–2

Then, six days before the Passover, Jesus came to Bethany, where Lazarus was who had been dead, whom He had raised from the dead. There they made Him a supper; and Martha served, but Lazarus was one of those who sat at the table with Him.

The Burden

Mark 11:1–11

Now when they drew near Jerusalem, to Bethphage and Bethany, at the Mount of Olives, He sent two of His disciples; and He said to them, "Go into the village opposite you; and as soon as you have entered it you will find a colt tied, on which no one has sat. Loose it and bring it." . . . Then they brought the colt to Jesus and threw their clothes on it, and He sat on it. And many spread their clothes on the road, and others cut down leafy branches from the trees and spread them on the road. Then those who went before and those who followed cried out, saying: "Hosanna! 'Blessed is He who comes in the name of the Lord!' Blessed is the kingdom of our father David that comes in the name of the Lord! Hosanna in the highest!" And Jesus went into Jerusalem and into the temple. So when He had looked around at all things, as the hour was already late, He went out to Bethany with the twelve.

Psalm 22:1, 7–8, 14–18

My God, My God, why have You forsaken Me? . . .

All those who see Me ridicule Me; They shoot out the lip, they shake the head, saying, "He trusted in the Lord, let Him rescue Him; Let Him deliver Him, since He delights in Him!". . .

I am poured out like water, and all My bones are out of joint; My heart is like wax; it has melted within Me. My strength is dried up like a potsherd, and My tongue clings to My jaws; You have brought Me to the dust of death. For dogs have surrounded Me; the congregation of the wicked has enclosed Me. They pierced My hands and My feet; I can count all My bones. They look and stare at Me. They divide My garments among them, and for My clothing they cast lots.

Psalm 69:19–21

You know my reproach, my shame, and my dishonor;
My adversaries are all before You.
Reproach has broken my heart,
And I am full of heaviness;
I looked for someone to take pity, but there was none;
And for comforters, but I found none.
They also gave me gall for my food,
And for my thirst they gave me vinegar to drink.

The Olive Press

Matthew 26:36–38

Then Jesus came with them to a place called Gethsemane, and said to the disciples, "Sit here while I go and pray over there." And He took with Him Peter and the two sons of Zebedee, and He began to be sorrowful and deeply distressed. Then He said to them, "My soul is exceedingly sorrowful, even to death."

Luke 22:44

And being in agony, He prayed more earnestly. Then His sweat became like great drops of blood falling down to the ground.

Note: Gethsemane is the Aramaic word for olive press.

The Scholar

And Jesus Stood

1 Peter 1:18–19

. . . knowing that you were not redeemed with corruptible things, like silver or gold . . . but with the precious blood of Christ, as of a lamb without blemish and without spot.

Hebrews 5:8–9

. . . though He was a Son, yet He learned obedience by the things which He suffered. And having been perfected, He became the author of eternal salvation to all who obey Him . . . .

Matthew 27:11 (KING JAMES VERSION)

And Jesus stood before the governor: and the governor asked Him, saying, Art thou the King of the Jews? And Jesus said unto him, Thou sayest.

Good Friday, 1987

Good Friday, Flying Eastward

Revelation 1:5–6

To Him who loved us and washed us from our sins in His own blood, and has made us kings and priests to His God and Father, to Him be glory and dominion forever and ever. Amen.

Luke 23:44–46

Now it was about the sixth hour, and there was darkness over all the earth until the ninth hour. Then the sun was darkened, and the veil of the temple was torn in two. And when Jesus had cried out with a loud voice, He said, "Father, 'into Your hands I commit My spirit.'" Having said this, He breathed His last.

Psalm 31:5

Into Your hand I commit my spirit; You have redeemed me, O LORD God of truth.

The Man Who Walked

Genesis 22:6–8

So Abraham took the wood of the burnt offering and laid it on Isaac his son; and he took the fire in his hand, and a knife, and the two of them went together. But Isaac spoke to Abraham his father and said, "My father!" And he said, "Here I am, my son." Then he said, "Look, the fire and the wood, but where is the lamb for a burnt offering?" And Abraham said, "My son, God will provide for Himself the lamb for a burnt offering." So the two of them went together.

Exodus 3:14

And God said to Moses, "I AM WHO I AM." And He said, "Thus you shall say to the children of Israel, 'I AM has sent me to you.'"

The Man Who Walked

Mark 14:61–62

But He kept silent and answered nothing. Again the high priest asked Him, saying to Him, "Are You the Christ, the Son of the Blessed?" Jesus said, "I am. And you will see the Son of Man sitting at the right hand of the Power, and coming with the clouds of heaven."

The Men Who Knew

Mark 12:7–8

"But those vinedressers said among themselves, 'This is the heir. Come, let us kill him, and the inheritance will be ours.' So they took him and killed him and cast him out of the vineyard."

The Signature

Luke 23:32–43

There were also two others, criminals, led with Him to be put to death. And when they had come to the place called Calvary, there they crucified Him, and the criminals, one on the right hand and the other on the left. Then Jesus said, "Father, forgive them, for they do not know what they do. . . ." But even the rulers with them sneered, saying, "He saved others; let Him save Himself if He is the Christ, the chosen of God. . . ." Then one of the criminals who were hanged blasphemed Him, saying, "If You are the Christ, save Yourself and us." But the other, answering, rebuked him, saying, "Do you not even fear God, seeing you are under the same condemnation? And we indeed justly, for we receive the due reward of our deeds; but this Man has done nothing wrong." Then he said to Jesus, "Lord, remember me when You come into Your kingdom." And Jesus said to him, "Assuredly, I say to you, today you will be with Me in Paradise."

The Signature

Matthew 20:1–9

"For the kingdom of heaven is like a landowner who went out early in the morning to hire laborers for his vineyard. Now when he had agreed with the laborers for a denarius a day, he sent them into his vineyard. . . . And about the eleventh hour he went out and found others standing idle, and said to them, 'Why have you been standing here idle all day?' They said to him, 'Because no one hired us.' He said to them, 'You also go into the vineyard, and whatever is right you will receive.' So when evening had come, the owner of the vineyard said to his steward, 'Call the laborers and give them their wages, beginning with the last to the first.' And when those came who were hired about the eleventh hour, they each received a denarius. . . ."

The Old Man's Prophecy

Luke 2:34–35

Then Simeon blessed them, and said to Mary His mother, "Behold, this Child is destined for the fall and rising of many in Israel, and for a sign which will be spoken against (yes, a sword will pierce through your own soul also), that the thoughts of many hearts may be revealed."

John 19:25–27

Now there stood by the cross of Jesus His mother, and His mother's sister, Mary the wife of Clopas, and Mary Magdalene. When Jesus therefore saw His mother, and the disciple whom He loved standing by, He said to His mother, "Woman, behold your son!" Then He said to the disciple, "Behold your mother!" And from that hour that disciple took her to his own home.

Keystone

John 19:28–30

After this, Jesus, knowing that all things were now accomplished, that the Scripture might be fulfilled, said, "I thirst!" Now a vessel full of sour wine was sitting there; and they filled a sponge with sour wine, put it on hyssop, and put it to His mouth. So when Jesus had received the sour wine, He said, "It is finished!" And bowing His head, He gave up His spirit.

The Witness

Mark 15:39

So when the centurion, who stood opposite Him, saw that He cried out like this and breathed His last, he said, "Truly this Man was the Son of God!"

Psalm 22:1, 7–8, 14–18

My God, My God, why have You forsaken Me? . . .
    All those who see Me ridicule Me; They shoot out the lip, they shake the head, saying, "He trusted in the Lord, let Him rescue Him; Let Him deliver Him, since He delights in Him!". . .
    I am poured out like water, and all My bones are out of joint; My heart is like wax; it has melted within Me. My strength is dried up like a potsherd, and My tongue clings to My jaws; You have brought Me to the dust of death. For dogs have surrounded Me; the congregation of the wicked has enclosed Me. They pierced My hands and My feet; I can count all My bones. They look and stare at Me. They divide My garments among them, and for My clothing they cast lots.

The Curtain

Matthew 27:41–51

Likewise the chief priests also, mocking with the scribes and elders, said, "He saved others; Himself He cannot save. If He is the King of Israel, let Him now come down from the cross, and we will believe Him. He trusted in God; let Him deliver Him now if He will have Him; for He said, 'I am the Son of God.'" Even the robbers who were crucified with Him reviled Him with the same thing. Now from the sixth hour until the ninth hour there was darkness over all the land. And about the ninth hour Jesus cried out with a loud voice, saying, "Eli, Eli, lama sabachthani?" that is, "My God, My God, why have You forsaken Me . . . . ?" And Jesus cried out again with a loud voice, and yielded up His spirit. Then, behold, the veil of the temple was torn in two from top to bottom . . . .

The Hiding Place

Isaiah 32:1–2

Behold, a king will reign in righteousness, . . .
A man will be as a hiding place from the wind,
And a cover from the tempest,
As rivers of water in a dry place,
As the shadow of a great rock in a weary land.

Where He Was Crucified

John 19:38–42

After this, Joseph of Arimathea, being a disciple of Jesus, but secretly, for fear of the Jews, asked Pilate that he might take away the body of Jesus; and Pilate gave him permission. So he came and took the body of Jesus. And Nicodemus, who at first came to Jesus by night, also came, bringing a mixture of myrrh and aloes, about a hundred pounds. Then they took the body of Jesus, and bound it in strips of linen with the spices, as the custom of the Jews is to bury. Now in the place where He was crucified there was a garden, and in the garden a new tomb in which no one had yet been laid. So there they laid Jesus, because of the Jews' Preparation Day, for the tomb was nearby.

I Lay in Darkness

Psalm 139:11–12

If I say, "Surely the darkness shall fall on me,"
Even the night shall be light about me;
Indeed, the darkness shall not hide from You,
But the night shines as the day;
The darkness and the light are both alike to You.

Deathwatch

Matthew 28:1–15

Now after the Sabbath, as the first day of the week began to dawn, Mary Magdalene and the other Mary came to see the tomb. And behold, there was a great earthquake; for an angel of the Lord descended from heaven, and came and rolled back the stone from the door, and sat on it. His countenance was like lightning, and his clothing as white as snow. And the guards shook for fear of him, and became like dead men. . . .

[Then] some of the guard came into the city and reported to the chief priests all the things that had happened. When they had assembled with the elders and consulted together, they gave a large sum of money to the soldiers, saying, "Tell them, 'His disciples came at night and stole Him away while we slept.' And if this comes to the governor's ears, we will appease him and make you secure." So they took the money and did as they were instructed; and this saying is commonly reported among the Jews until this day.

Who Told Saint Matthew?

Matthew 28:2

And behold, there was a great earthquake; for an angel of the Lord descended from heaven, and came and rolled back the stone from the door, and sat on it.

Genesis 8:8–9

[Noah] also sent out from himself a dove, to see if the waters had receded from the face of the ground. But the dove found no resting place for the sole of her foot, and she returned into the ark to him, for the waters were on the face of the whole earth. So he put out his hand and took her, and drew her into the ark to himself.

Who Told Saint Matthew?

Book of Common Prayer
Collect for the Second Sunday in Advent

Blessed Lord, who hast caused all holy Scriptures to be written for our learning; Grant that we may in such wise hear them, read, mark, learn, and inwardly digest them, that by patience and comfort of thy holy Word, we may embrace, and ever hold fast, the blessed hope of everlasting life, which thou hast given us in our Saviour Jesus Christ. Amen.

I Did Not Weep

John 20:11-16

But Mary stood outside by the tomb weeping, and as she wept she stooped down and looked into the tomb. And she saw two angels in white sitting, one at the head and the other at the feet, where the body of Jesus had lain. Then they said to her, "Woman, why are you weeping?" She said to them, "Because they have taken away my Lord, and I do not know where they have laid Him." Now when she had said this, she turned around and saw Jesus standing there, and did not know that it was Jesus. Jesus said to her, "Woman, why are you weeping? Whom are you seeking?" She, supposing Him to be the gardener, said to Him, "Sir, if You have carried Him away, tell me where You have laid Him, and I will take Him away." Jesus said to her, "Mary!"

The Bible Study (I) and
The Bible Study (II)

Luke 24:13-33

Now behold, two of them were traveling that same day to a village called Emmaus, which was seven miles from Jerusalem. And they talked together of all these things which had happened.

So it was, while they conversed and reasoned, that Jesus Himself drew near and went with them. But their eyes were restrained, so that they did not know Him. And He said to them, "What kind of conversation is this that you have with one another as you walk and are sad?" Then the one whose name was Cleopas answered and said to Him, "Are You the only stranger in Jerusalem, and have You not known the things which happened there in these days?" And He said to them, "What things?"

So they said to Him, "The things concerning Jesus of Nazareth, who was a Prophet mighty in deed and word before God and all the people, and how the chief priests and our rulers delivered Him to be condemned to death, and crucified Him. But we were hoping that it was He who was going to redeem Israel. Indeed, besides all this, today is the third day since these things happened. Yes, and certain women of our company, who arrived at the tomb early, astonished us. When they did not find His body, they came saying that they had also seen a vision of angels who said He was alive. And certain of those who were with us went to the tomb and found it just as the women had said; but Him they did not see."

Then He said to them, "O foolish ones, and slow of heart to believe in all that the prophets have spoken! Ought not the Christ to have suffered these things and to enter into His glory?" And beginning at Moses and all the Prophets, He expounded to them in all the Scriptures the things concerning Himself.

Then they drew near to the village where they were going, and He indicated that He would have gone farther. But they constrained Him, saying, "Abide with us, for it is toward evening, and the day is far spent." And He went in to stay with them. Now it came to pass, as He sat at the table with them, that He took bread, blessed and broke it, and gave it to them. Then their eyes were opened and they knew Him; and He vanished from their sight. And they said to one another, "Did not our heart burn within us while He talked with us on the road, and while He opened the Scriptures to us?" So they rose up that very hour and returned to Jerusalem . . . .

The Epithet

John 20:24-29

Now Thomas, called the Twin, one of the twelve, was not with them when Jesus came. The other disciples therefore said to him, "We have seen the Lord." So he said to them, "Unless I see in His hands the print of the nails, and put my finger into the print of the nails, and put my hand into His side, I will not believe."

And after eight days His disciples were again inside, and Thomas with them. Jesus came, the doors being shut, and stood in the midst, and said, "Peace to you!"

Then He said to Thomas, "Reach your finger here, and look at My hands; and reach your hand here, and put it into My side. Do not be unbelieving, but believing."

And Thomas answered and said to Him, "My Lord and my God!"

Jesus said to him, "Thomas, because you have seen Me, you have believed. Blessed are those who have not seen and yet have believed."

About the Poet

Philip Brown Rosenbaum became a Christian in his mid-twenties and wrote his first poem at the age of thirty-four. He was born and raised in Washington, D.C. where he attended St. Albans School and sang in the Choir of Men and Boys at the Washington National Cathedral. He earned a degree in English at Harvard, then worked with delinquent boys as a counselor and school director before being called to an evangelical ministry in California. His previous books, both prose works, are *How to Enjoy the Boring Parts of the Bible* and *The Promise*. Currently a fine arts consultant, he lives in rural Virginia with his wife, Jeanne, and their five children.

COLOPHON

Holy Week Sonnets was designed by Kathleen Sims
of Sims Design Company, Washington, D.C.
The first edition was printed offset
on 80# Mohawk Tomahawk and bound by
Sheridan Books, Ann Arbor, Michigan.

The type throughout is the antique
and traditionally popular Janson,
with ornamental lettering in Galahad,
a new face designed by Alan Blackman.

The typographic decorations below the poems
represent traditional symbols in the Christian
visual lexicon. In order of their appearance in the
book, they are: laurel symbolizing triumph; palm,
spiritual victory and Jesus's entry into Jerusalem;
holly, the passion of Christ; clover, the trinity;
daisy, innocence; thistle, earthly sorrow;
ivy, life eternal; wheat, bounty.